D0540742

TRAILING CLOUDS of GLORY

Poems by William Wordsworth

William West   A Mountainous Landscape with a Rocky Pool

TRAILING CLOUDS
of GLORY

Poems by William Wordsworth

SELECTED AND WITH AN INTRODUCTION BY PAMELA TODD

PAVILION

For my Mother and Father,
With Love

First published in Great Britain in 1996 by
PAVILION BOOKS LIMITED
26 Upper Ground, London SE1 9PD

Introduction copyright © Pamela Todd 1996
Compilation and design copyright © David Fordham and Pamela Todd 1996

All rights reserved. No part of this publication may be reproduced, stored in a retrieval
system, or transmitted, in any form or by any means, electronic, mechanical,
photocopying, recording or otherwise, without the prior permission of the copyright
holder

A CIP catalogue record for this book is available from the British Library

ISBN 1 85793 649 3

Designed by David Fordham
Typeset in Helvetica Bold and Garamond Light by SX Composing Ltd, Rayleigh
Printed and bound in Italy by Graphicom

2 4 6 8 10 9 7 5 3 1

This book may be ordered by post direct from the publisher.
Please contact the Marketing Department. But try your bookshop first.

Contents

Henry Moore   GOWBARROW PARK, ULLSWATER

TRAILING CLOUDS *of* GLORY

WILLIAM WORDSWORTH'S DEEP LOVE OF NATURE AND OF FREEDOM IS MIRRORED IN his poetry. He had an eye for the wide, windy sweep of sky, the vast surface of the lake, but also for the 'homely face' of the daisy or the perfect poise of a butterfly. He looked to nature for truth, beauty, serenity, joy and education:

> Books! 'tis dull and endless strife:
> Come, hear the woodland linnet,
> How sweet his music! on my life
> There's more of wisdom in it

he urges in 'The Tables Turned' and, in 'To My Sister' he declares that:

> One moment now may give us more
> Than fifty years of reason;
> Our minds shall drink at every pore
> The spirit of the season.

Nature was, to Wordsworth, absolutely central. He had grown up in the wild mountain country between Windermere and Coniston, an energetic young boy, daring and adventurous. He spent much of his time out of doors, walking by day and by night, climbing, skating, nutting, flying kites, boating and fishing, and delighting in the immensity and beauty of his natural surroundings. In his great poetic autobiography, *The Prelude*, he writes of how, as a child, he imagined he heard the moorlands breathing on his neck; how, when nutting, he found 'there was a spirit in the woods'; and of the time when he rowed out at night in a stolen boat on an unfamiliar lake and was shaken by the vision of a vast mountain peak, which seemed to stride after him, so that his mind was haunted by the sense of 'unknown modes of being'. These early experiences struck deep and shaped his poetic temperament. Nature, he wrote in *The Prelude*:

> Peopled my mind with beauteous forms and grand.

His character – strong, stubborn at times, often austere but tempered by a tenderness for friends and family – was formed by the vastness of his surroundings:

> these steep and lofty cliffs,
> That on a wild secluded scene impress
> Thoughts of more deep seclusion; and connect
> The landscape with the quiet of the sky.

These lines come from 'Tintern Abbey', an intimate, meditative exploration of personal experience – the return after a gap of five years, with his sister, to a place of beauty and former resonance – and an extraordinary imaginative response to nature. The tone is carefully modulated, controlled, yet confiding, urgent and intense. Wordsworth had a remarkable unity of spirit with his younger sister, Dorothy, whose gentle love of nature tamed his wilder, boisterous side. They took long walks together, or:

> Lay listening to the wild flowers and the grass

and his respect for nature grew. 'I would not strike a flower,' he wrote, and if by chance he kicked a tuft of 'meadow lilies' or snapped a foxglove stem, he would stop:

> Self-questioned, asking wherefore that was done.

Solitude and space were important to him but set against the reassuring and harmonious background of a serene domestic household, presided over first by his devoted Dorothy:

> My Sister! ('tis a wish of mine)
> Now that our morning meal is done,
> Make haste, your morning task resign:
> Come forth and feel the sun

and, after 1802, by his no less devoted wife, Mary Hutchinson.

As early as fourteen he had begun to collect 'images of nature' and at sixteen he was shaping them into poetry. By the time he left Cambridge – where he complained of feeling like 'a fowl of the air, ill-tutored for captivity' – poetry was an important part of his life, but he lacked means and his guardians (his mother had died when he was eight, his father when he was thirteen) urged him to enter one of the professions. Instead he drifted, 'seeing life' as he called it. He spent two years in France [1791-2] during what was perhaps the most intensely exciting period of the Revolution:

> Bliss was it in that dawn to be alive,
> But to be young was very heaven.

He was young, radical, revolutionary and in love. He had an affair with Annette Vallon, the daughter of Royalist parents and they had a child, which Wordsworth acknowledged at her christening, but politics and war intervened before they could marry. Over time his love faded under the pressure of absence, from passion into sorrow and self-blame, until finally:

> memory of what hath been
> And never more can be.

At a highly charged moment in his life, he and Dorothy, taking advantage of the temporary peace of Amiens in 1802, slipped across the channel to Calais to see Annette and her daughter Caroline for the first time in ten years. William had already determined to marry Mary Hutchinson, an old friend of their childhood, and it seems he went to make his peace with Annette and settle money on the child.

In the intervening years he had at first roamed restlessly, much troubled in his mind, the guest or companion of friends, until in 1795 – on the edge of what we would now term a nervous breakdown – he was saved from financial anxiety by the generous act of a dying friend, Raisley Calvert, who left him a legacy of £900 to enable him to pursue his vocation as a poet. A new period of great stability and domestic harmony now opened up for Wordsworth. He and Dorothy were able to realize their long cherished dream of setting up home together, first at Racedown in Dorset, and then at Alfoxden in Somerset, where they moved after a year to be closer to Samuel Taylor Coleridge.

Coleridge and Dorothy were, Wordsworth claimed, the two people to whom his intellect owed the most. The two poets were engaged in one of the most fruitful poetic collaborations of all time. *Lyrical Ballads* (the title itself was a challenge to the literary establishment) was published in 1798 and much of the charm of the poems, which has endured now for almost two hundred years, comes from their openness and apparent simplicity. Instinct, emotion and imagination were truer to Wordsworth than 'meddling intellect' and by 'looking steadily' at his subject he succeeding in describing the quiet dignity of the rural communities he observed around him and exploring questions of morality and the nature of good and evil. It may be difficult now to recognize just how revolutionary the book was in its time. In his preface (which has come to be studied with almost as much attention as the poems) Wordsworth set out his intention to move away from the high-flown rhetoric of the eighteenth-century neo-classicism and return to 'the real language of men':

> There will also be found in these volumes little of what is usually called poetic diction; I have taken as much pains to avoid it as others ordinarily take to produce it; this I have done for the reason already alleged, to bring my language near to the language of men, and further because the pleasure which I have proposed to myself to impart is of a kind very different from that which is supposed by many persons to be the proper object of poetry.

The peace of the countryside had restored his mental health but he began to yearn for the wild landscapes of his youth and in December 1799 Dorothy and William settled in Dove Cottage, Grasmere, so celebrated in his poems, particularly in 'Farewell, Thou Little Nook of Mountain Ground'. They were not well off though they were able to afford a few luxuries – tea, a newspaper – which added to the quality and serenity of their life at this time. It was a particularly happy and productive period for Wordsworth and the harmony and compatibility of his domestic arrangements were the envy of Coleridge, who was a frequent visitor. The friends took long walks in all weathers and Dorothy recorded her impressions in a journal kept expressly to help William. Many of Wordsworth's poems of this time are connected with Dorothy in some way. Some, like 'To a Butterfly' record incidents of their childhood; many reflect Dorothy's interest in flowers and smaller birds – 'The Green Linnet', 'To a Sky-Lark', 'To the Small Celandine' and 'The Sparrow's Nest'. It is clear that these charming poems were written to please her.

Wordsworth was to live in the parish of Grasmere for the rest of his life, writing steadily, though without ever recapturing the bold originality of his early golden period. His writing career was long and distinguished and he remained always alive to the beauty and mystery of nature. The visionary states which he used to fear had gone and now he found he missed their 'dreamlike vividness and splendour'. In 1813 he moved into Rydal Mount, where he lived with Mary and their children (they had five, though two died), serenely for the most part, though his final years were darkened by Dorothy's mental breakdown. In 1843 he was made Poet Laureate and he held the post until his death on 23 April 1850. He was in his eightieth year.

PAMELA TODD 1996

A **SLUMBER DID MY SPIRIT SEAL;**
>I had no human fears:
>She seemed a thing that could not feel
>>The touch of earthly years.

>No motion has she now, no force;
>>She neither hears nor sees,
>Rolled round in earth's diurnal course
>>With rocks and stones and trees.

Daniel Alexander Williamson   Spring, Arnside Knot and Coniston Range of Hills from Warton Crag

William James Blacklock   Catbells and Causey Pike

LINES LEFT UPON A SEAT IN A YEW-TREE

WHICH STANDS NEAR THE LAKE OF

ESTHWAITE, ON A DESOLATE PART OF THE

SHORE, YET COMMANDING A BEAUTIFUL

PROSPECT

NAY, TRAVELLER! REST. THIS LONELY
YEW-TREE STANDS

Far from all human dwelling: what if here
No sparkling rivulet spread the verdant herb;
What if these barren boughs the bee not loves;
Yet, if the wind breathe soft, the curling waves,
That break against the shore, shall lull thy mind
By one soft impulse saved from vacancy.

——————Who he was
That piled these stones, and with the mossy sod
First covered o'er, and taught this aged tree,
Now wild, to bend its arms in circling shade,
I well remember. – He was one who owned
No common soul. In youth, by genius nursed,
And big with lofty views, he to the world
Went forth, pure in his heart, against the taint
Of dissolute tongues, 'gainst jealousy, and hate,

And scorn, against all enemies prepared,
All but neglect: and so, his spirit damped
At once, with rash disdain he turned away,
And with the food of pride sustained his soul
In solitude. – Stranger! these gloomy boughs
Had charms for him; and here he loved to sit,
His only visitants a straggling sheep,
The stone-chat, or the glancing sand-piper;
And on these barren rocks, with juniper,
And heath, and thistle, thinly sprinkled o'er,
Fixing his downward eye, he many an hour
A morbid pleasure nourished, tracing here
An emblem of his own unfruitful life:
And lifting up his head, he then would gaze
On the more distant scene; how lovely 'tis
Thou seest, and he would gaze till it became
Far lovelier, and his heart could not sustain

The beauty still more beauteous. Nor, that time,
Would he forget those beings, to whose minds,
Warm from the labours of benevolence,
The world, and man himself, appeared a scene
Of kindred loveliness: then he would sigh
With mournful joy, to think that others felt
What he must never feel: and so, lost man!
On visionary views would fancy feed,
Till his eye streamed with tears. In this deep vale
He died, this seat his only monument.

If thou be one whose heart the holy forms
Of young imagination have kept pure,
Stranger! henceforth be warned; and know, that pride,

Howe'er disguised in its own majesty,
Is littleness; that he, who feels contempt
For any living thing, hath faculties
Which he has never used; that thought with him
Is in its infancy. The man, whose eye
Is ever on himself, doth look on one,
The least of nature's works, one who might move
The wise man to that scorn which wisdom holds
Unlawful, ever. O, be wiser thou!
Instructed that true knowledge leads to love,
True dignity abides with him alone
Who, in the silent hour of inward thought,
Can still suspect, and still revere himself,
In lowliness of heart.

W H Watson   Pastoral Landscape

Joseph Mallord William Turner   THE WOODWALK, FARNLEY HALL 1818

IT IS THE FIRST MILD DAY OF MARCH:
Each minute sweeter than before,
The red-breast sings from the tall larch
That stands beside our door.

There is a blessing in the air,
Which seems a sense of joy to yield
To the bare trees, and mountains bare,
And grass in the green field.

My Sister! ('tis a wish of mine)
Now that our morning meal is done,
Make haste, your morning task resign;
Come forth and feel the sun.

Edward will come with you, and pray,
Put on with speed your woodland dress,
And bring no book, for this one day
We'll give to idleness.

No joyless forms shall regulate
Our living Calendar:
We from to-day, my friend, will date
The opening of the year.

Love, now an universal birth,
From heart to heart is stealing,
From earth to man, from man to earth,
– It is the hour of feeling.

One moment now may give us more
Than fifty years of reason;
Our minds shall drink at every pore
The spirit of the season.

Some silent laws our hearts may make,
Which they shall long obey;
We for the year to come may take
Our temper from to-day.

And from the blessed power that rolls
About, below, above;
We'll frame the measure of our souls
They shall be tuned to love.

Then come, my sister! come, I pray,
With speed put on your woodland dress,
And bring no book; for this one day
We'll give to idleness.

Goody Blake and Harry Gill

A True Story

OH! WHAT'S THE MATTER? WHAT'S THE MATTER?
What is't that ails young Harry Gill?
That evermore his teeth they chatter,
Chatter, chatter, chatter still.
Of waistcoats Harry has no lack,
Good duffle grey, and flannel fine;
He has a blanket on his back
And coats enough to smother nine.

In March, December, and in July,
'Tis all the same with Harry Gill;
The neighbours tell, and tell you truly,
His teeth they chatter, chatter still.
At night, at morning, and at noon,
'Tis all the same with Harry Gill;
Beneath the sun, beneath the moon,
His teeth they chatter, chatter still.

Young Harry was a lusty drover,
And who so stout of limb as he?
His cheeks were red as ruddy clover,
His voice was like the voice of three.

Auld Goody Blake was old and poor,
Ill fed she was, and thinly clad;
And any man who passed her door,
Might see how poor a hut she had.

All day she spun in her poor dwelling,
And then her three hours' work at night!
Alas! 'twas hardly worth the telling,
It would not pay for candle-light.
– This woman dwelt in Dorsetshire,
Her hut was on a cold hill-side,
And in that country coals are dear,
For they come far by wind and tide.

By the same fire to boil their pottage,
Two poor old dames, as I have known,
Will often live in one small cottage,
But she, poor woman, dwelt alone.
'Twas well enough when summer came,
The long, warm, lightsome summer-day,
Then at her door the *canty* dame
Would sit, as any linnet gay.

Caroline Williams   WINTER'S EVENING

But when the ice our streams did fetter,
Oh! then how her old bones would shake!
You would have said, if you had met her,
'Twas a hard time for Goody Blake.
Her evenings then were dull and dead;
Sad case it was, as you may think,
For very cold to go to bed,
And then for cold not sleep a wink.

Oh joy for her! when e'er in winter
The winds at night had made a rout,
And scattered many a lusty splinter,
And many a rotten bough about.
Yet never had she, well or sick,
As every man who knew her says,
A pile before-hand, wood or stick,
Enough to warm her for three days.

Now, when the frost was past enduring,
And made her poor old bones to ache,
Could any thing be more alluring,
Than an old hedge to Goody Blake?
And now and then, it must be said,
When her old bones were cold and chill,

She left her fire, or left her bed,
To seek the hedge of Harry Gill.

Now Harry he had long suspected
This trespass of old Goody Blake,
And vowed that she should be detected,
And he on her would vengeance take.
And oft from his warm fire he'd go,
And to the fields his road would take,
And there, at night, in frost and snow,
He watched to seize old Goody Blake.

And once, behind a rick of barley,
Thus looking out did Harry stand;
The moon was full and shining clearly,
And crisp with frost the stubble-land.
– He hears a noise – he's all awake –
Again? – on tip-toe down the hill
He softly creeps – 'Tis Goody Blake,
She's at the hedge of Harry Gill.

Right glad was he when he beheld her:
Stick after stick did Goody pull,
He stood behind a bush of elder,
Till she had filled her apron full.

When with her load she turned about,
The bye-road back again to take
He started forward with a shout,
And sprang upon poor Goody Blake.

And fiercely by the arm he took her,
And by the arm he held her fast,
And fiercely by the arm he shook her,
And cried, 'I've caught you then at last!'
Then Goody, who had nothing said,
Her bundle from her lap let fall;
And kneeling on the sticks, she prayed
To God that is the judge of all.

She prayed, her withered hand uprearing,
While Harry held her by the arm –
'God! who art never out of hearing,
Oh may he never more be warm!'
The cold, cold moon above her head,
Thus on her knees did Goody pray,
Young Harry heard what she had said,
And icy-cold he turned away.

He went complaining all the morrow
That he was cold and very chill:

His face was gloom, his heart was sorrow,
Alas! that day for Harry Gill!
That day he wore a riding-coat,
But not a whit the warmer he:
Another was on Thursday brought,
And ere the Sabbath he had three.

'Twas all in vain, a useless matter,
And blankets were about him pinned;
Yet still his jaws and teeth they clatter,
Like a loose casement in the wind.
And Harry's flesh it fell away;
And all who see him say 'tis plain,
That, live as long as live he may,
He never will be warm again.

No word to any man he utters,
A-bed or up, to young or old;
But ever to himself he mutters,
'Poor Harry Gill is very cold.'
A-bed or up, by night or day;
His teeth they chatter, chatter still.
Now think, ye farmers all, I pray,
Of Goody Blake and Harry Gill.

I HEARD A THOUSAND BLENDED NOTES,
While in a grove I sate reclined,
In that sweet mood when pleasant thoughts
Bring sad thoughts to the mind.

To her fair works did Nature link
The human soul that through me ran;
And much it grieved my heart to think
What man has made of man.

Through primrose-tufts, in that green bower,
The periwinkle trailed its wreathes;
And 'tis my faith that every flower
Enjoys the air it breathes.

The birds around me hopped and played:
Their thoughts I cannot measure,
But the least motion which they made,
It seemed a thrill of pleasure.

The budding twigs spread out their fan,
To catch the breezy air;
And I must think, do all I can,
That there was pleasure there.

If this belief from heaven be sent,
If such be Nature's holy plan,
Have I not reason to lament
What man has made of man?

John Wainwright PRIMROSE AND ROBIN

William Havell WINDERMERE

WHY WILLIAM, ON THAT OLD GREY STONE,
Thus for the length of half a day,
Why William, sit you thus alone,
And dream your time away?

'Where are your books? that light bequeathed
To beings else forlorn and blind!
Up! Up! and drink the spirit breathed
From dead men to their kind.

'You look round on your Mother Earth,
As if she for no purpose bore you;
As if you were her first-born birth,
And none had lived before you!'

One morning thus, by Esthwaite lake,
When life was sweet I knew not why,
To me my good friend Matthew spake,
And thus I made reply.

'The eye it cannot chuse but see,
We cannot bid the ear be still;
Our bodies feel, where'er they be,
Against, or with our will.

'Nor less I deem that there are Powers,
Which of themselves our minds impress,
That we can feed this mind of ours,
In a wise passiveness.

'Think you, 'mid all this mighty sum
Of things for ever speaking,
That nothing of itself will come,
But we must still be seeking?

'– Then ask not wherefore, here, alone,
Conversing as I may,
I sit upon this old grey stone,
And dream my time away.'

AN EVENING SCENE, ON THE SAME SUBJECT

UP! UP! MY FRIEND, AND QUIT YOUR BOOKS,
Or surely you'll grow double.
Up! up! my friend, and clear your looks,
Why all this toil and trouble?

The sun above the mountain's head,
A freshening lustre mellow,
Through all the long green fields has spread,
His first sweet evening yellow.

Books! 'tis a dull and endless strife,
Come, hear the woodland linnet,
How sweet his music; on my life
There's more of wisdom in it.

And hark! how blithe the throstle sings!
He, too, is no mean preacher;
Come forth into the light of things,
Let Nature be your Teacher.

She has a world of ready wealth,
Our minds and hearts to bless –
Spontaneous wisdom breathed by health,
Truth breathed by chearfulness.

One impulse from a vernal wood
May teach you more of man;
Of moral evil and of good,
Than all the sages can.

Sweet is the lore which Nature brings;
Our meddling intellect
Mis-shapes the beauteous forms of things;
– We murder to dissect.

Enough of Science and of Art;
Close up these barren leaves;
Come forth, and bring with you a heart
That watches and receives.

LINES COMPOSED A FEW MILES ABOVE TINTERN ABBEY

ON REVISITING THE BANKS OF THE WYE DURING

A TOUR. JULY 13, 1798.

FIVE YEARS HAVE PAST; FIVE SUMMERS,
WITH THE LENGTH
Of five long winters! and again I hear
These waters, rolling from their mountain-springs
With a soft inland murmur. – Once again
Do I behold these steep and lofty cliffs,
That on a wild secluded scene impress
Thoughts of more deep seclusion; and connect
The landscape with the quiet of the sky.
The day is come when I again repose
Here, under this dark sycamore, and view
These plots of cottage-ground, these orchard-tufts,
Which at this season, with their unripe fruits,
Are clad in one green hue, and lose themselves
'Mid groves and copses. Once again I see
These hedge-rows, hardly hedge-rows, little lines
Of sportive wood run wild: these pastoral farms,
Green to the very door; and wreaths of smoke
Sent up, in silence, from among the trees!

With some uncertain notice, as might seem
Of vagrant dwellers in the houseless woods,
Or of some Hermit's cave, where by his fire
The Hermit sits alone.

              These beauteous forms,
Through a long absence, have not been to me
As is a landscape to a blind man's eye:
But oft, in lonely rooms, and 'mid the din
Of towns and cities, I have owed to them,
In hours of weariness, sensations sweet,
Felt in the blood, and felt along the heart;
And passing even into my purer mind,
With tranquil restoration: – feelings too
Of unremembered pleasure: such, perhaps,
As have no slight or trivial influence
On that best portion of a good man's life,
His little, nameless, unremembered, acts
Of kindness and of love. Nor less, I trust,

To them I may have owed another gift.
Of aspect more sublime; that blessed mood,
In which the burthen of the mystery,
In which the heavy and the weary weight
Of all this unintelligible world,
Is lightened: – that serene and blessed mood,
In which the affections gently lead us on, –
Until, the breath of this corporeal frame
And even the motion of our human blood
Almost suspended, we are laid asleep
In body, and become a living soul:
While with an eye made quiet by the power
Of harmony, and the deep power of joy,
We see into the life of things.

                              If this
Be but a vain belief, yet, oh! how oft –
In darkness and amid the many shapes
Of joyless daylight; when the fretful stir
Unprofitable, and the fever of the world,
Have hung upon the beatings of my heart –
How oft, in spirit, have I turned to thee,
O sylvan Wye! thou wanderer thro' the woods,
How often has my spirit turned to thee!

And now, with gleams of half-extinguished thought,
With many recognitions dim and faint,
And somewhat of a sad perplexity,
The picture of the mind revives again:
While here I stand, not only with the sense
Of present pleasure, but with pleasing thoughts
That in this moment there is life and food
For future years. And so I dare to hope,
Though changed, no doubt, from what I was when first
I came among these hills; when like a roe
I bounded o'er the mountains, by the sides
Of the deep rivers, and the lonely streams,
Wherever nature led: more like a man
Flying from something that he dreads than one
Who sought the thing he loved. For nature then
(The coarser pleasures of my boyish days,
And their glad animal movements all gone by)
To me was all in all. – I cannot paint
What then I was. The sounding cataract
Haunted me like a passion: the tall rook,
The mountain, and the deep and gloomy wood,
Their colours and their forms, were then to me
An appetite; a feeling and a love,
That had no need of a remoter charm,

Harry Sutton Palmer   FROM THE WINDCLIFFE – THE JUNCTION OF THE WYE AND SEVERN

Joseph Mallord William Turner THE VALLEY OF THE WASHBURN

By thought supplied, nor any interest
Unborrowed from the eye. – That time is past,
And all its aching joys are now no more,
And all its dizzy raptures. Not for this
Faint I, nor mourn nor murmur; other gifts
Have followed; for such loss, I would believe,
Abundant recompense. For I have learned
To look on nature, not as in the hour
Of thoughtless youth; but hearing oftentimes
The still, sad music of humanity,
Nor harsh nor grating, though of ample power
To chasten and subdue. And I have felt
A presence that disturbs me with the joy
Of elevated thoughts; a sense sublime
Of something far more deeply interfused,
Whose dwelling is the light of setting suns,
And the round ocean and the living air,
And the blue sky, and in the mind of man:
A motion and a spirit, that impels
All thinking things, all objects of all thought,
And rolls through all things. Therefore am I still
A lover of the meadows and the woods,
And mountains; and of all that we behold
From this green earth; of all the mighty world

Of eye, and ear, – both what they half create,
And what perceive; well pleased to recognise
In nature and the language of the sense
The anchor of my purest thoughts, the nurse,
The guide, the guardian of my heart, and soul
Of all my moral being.

            Nor perchance,
If I were not thus taught, should I the more
Suffer my genial spirits to decay:
For thou art with me here upon the banks
Of this fair river; thou my dearest Friend,
My dear, dear Friend; and in thy voice I catch
The language of my former heart, and read
My former pleasures in the shooting lights
Of thy wild eyes. Oh! yet a little while
May I behold in thee what I was once,
My dear, dear Sister! and this prayer I make,
Knowing that Nature never did betray
The heart that loved her; 'tis her privilege,
Through all the years of this our life, to lead
From joy to joy: for she can so inform
The mind that is within us, so impress
With quietness and beauty, and so feed

With lofty thoughts, that neither evil tongues,
Rash judgments, nor the sneers of selfish men,
Nor greetings where no kindness is, nor all
The dreary intercourse of daily life,
Shall e'er prevail against us, or disturb
Our cheerful faith, that all which we behold
Is full of blessings. Therefore let the moon
Shine on thee in thy solitary walk;
And let the misty mountain-winds be free
To blow against thee: and, in after years,
When these wild ecstasies shall be matured
Into a sober pleasure; when thy mind
Shall be a mansion for all lovely forms,
Thy memory be as a dwelling-place
For all sweet sounds and harmonies; oh! then,

If solitude, or fear, or pain, or grief,
Should be thy portion, with what healing thoughts
Of tender joy wilt thou remember me,
And these my exhortations! Nor, perchance –
If I should be where I no more can hear
Thy voice, nor catch from thy wild eyes these
  gleams
Of past existence – wilt thou then forget
That on the banks of this delightful stream
We stood together; and that I, so long
A worshipper of Nature, hither came
Unwearied in that service: rather say
With warmer love – oh! with far deeper zeal
Of holier love. Nor wilt thou then forget
That after many wanderings, many years
Of absence, these steep woods and lofty cliffs,
And this green pastoral landscape, were to me
More dear, both for themselves and for thy sake!

WITH LITTLE HERE TO DO OR SEE
Of things that in the great world be,
Sweet Daisy! oft I talk to thee,
        For thou art worthy,
Thou unassuming Common-place
Of Nature, with that homely face,
And yet with something of a grace,
        Which Love makes for thee!

Oft do I sit by thee at ease,
And weave a web of similies,
Loose types of Things through all degrees,
        Thoughts of thy raising:
And many a fond and idle name
I give to thee, for praise or blame,
As is the humour of the game,
        While I am gazing.

A Nun demure of lowly port,
Or sprightly Maiden of Love's Court,
In thy simplicity the sport
        Of all temptations;
A Queen in crown of rubies drest,
A Starveling in a scanty vest,
Are all, as seem to suit thee best,
        Thy appellations.

A little Cyclops, with one eye
Staring to threaten and defy,
That thought comes next – and instantly
        The freak is over,
The shape will vanish, and behold!
A silver Shield with boss of gold,
That spreads itself, some Faery bold
        In fight to cover.

I see thee glittering from afar; –
And then thou art a pretty Star,
Not quite so fair as many are
        In heaven above thee!
Yet like a star, with glittering crest,
Self-poised in air thou seem'st to rest; –
May peace come never to this nest,
        Who shall reprove thee!

Sweet Flower! for by that name at last,
When all my reveries are past,
I call thee, and to that cleave fast,
        Sweet silent Creature!
That breath'st with me in sun and air,
Do thou, as thou art wont, repair
My heart with gladness, and a share
        Of thy meek nature!

OLD MAN TRAVELLING

ANIMAL **T**RANQUILLITY AND **D**ECAY, **A** **S**KETCH

THE LITTLE HEDGE-ROW BIRDS,

That peck along the road, regard him not.

He travels on, and in his face, his step,

His gait, is one expression; every limb,

His look and bending figure, all bespeak

A man who does not move with pain, but moves

With thought – He is insensibly subdued

To settled quiet: he is one by whom

All effort seems forgotten, one to whom

Long patience has such mild composure given,

That patience now doth seem a thing, of which

He hath no need. He is by nature led

To peace so perfect, that the young behold

With envy, what the old man hardly feels.

– I asked him whither he was bound, and what

The object of his journey; he replied

'Sir! I am going many miles to take

A last leave of my son, a mariner,

Who from a sea-fight has been brought to Falmouth,

And there is dying in an hospital.'

Sir Edwin Landseer   A**N** O**LD** M**AN AND HIS** D**OG** S**EATED BY A** R**OADSIDE**

LINES COMPOSED AT GRASMERE

During a Walk, one Evening, After a
Stormy Day, the Author Having just Read
in a Newspaper that the Dissolution of
Mr. Fox was Hourly Expected.

LOUD IS THE VALE! THE VOICE IS UP
With which she speaks when storms are gone,
A mighty Unison of streams!
Of all her Voices, One!

Loud is the Vale; – this inland Depth
In peace is roaring like the Sea;
Yon Star upon the mountain-top
Is listening quietly.

Sad was I, ev'n to pain depressed,
Importunate and heavy load!
The Comforter hath found me here,
Upon this lonely road;

And many thousands now are sad,
Wait the fulfilment of their fear;
For He must die who is their Stay,
Their Glory disappear.

A Power is passing from the earth
To breathless Nature's dark abyss;
But when the Mighty pass away
What is it more than this,

That Man, who is from God sent forth,
Doth yet again to God return? –
Such ebb and flow must ever be,
Then wherefore should we mourn?

Henry Gastineau   GRASMERE

NUTTING

It SEEMS A DAY,

One of those heavenly days which cannot die,
When forth I sallied from our cottage-door,
And with a wallet o'er my shoulder slung,
A nutting crook in hand, I turned my steps
Towards the distant woods, a Figure quaint,
Tricked out in proud disguise of Beggar's weeds
Put on for the occasion, by advice
And exhortation of my frugal Dame.
Motley accoutrements! of power to smile
At thorns, and brakes, and brambles, and, in truth,
More ragged than need was. Among the woods,
And o'er the pathless rocks, I forced my way
Until, at length, I came to one dear nook
Unvisited, where not a broken bough
Drooped with its withered leaves, ungracious sign
Of devastation, but the hazels rose
Tall and erect, with milk-white clusters hung,
A virgin scene! – A little while I stood,
Breathing with such suppression of the heart
As joy delights in; and with wise restraint

Voluptuous, fearless of a rival, eyed
The banquet, or beneath the trees I sate
Among the flowers, and with the flowers I played;
A temper known to those, who, after long
And weary expectation, have been blessed
With sudden happiness beyond all hope. –
– Perhaps it was a bower beneath whose leaves
The violets of five seasons re-appear
And fade, unseen by any human eye,
Where fairy water-breaks do murmur on
For ever, and I saw the sparkling foam,
And with my cheek on one of those green stones
That, fleeced with moss, beneath the shady trees,
Lay round me scattered like a flock of sheep,
I heard the murmur and the murmuring sound,
In that sweet mood when pleasure loves to pay
Tribute to ease, and, of its joy secure
The heart luxuriates with indifferent things,
Wasting its kindliness on stocks and stones,
And on the vacant air. Then up I rose,
And dragged to earth both branch and bough, with
   crash
And merciless ravage; and the shady nook
Of hazels, and the green and mossy bower,
Deformed and sullied, patiently gave up

Richard Redgrave   THE WOODLAND MIRROR

Their quiet being: and unless I now
Confound my present feelings with the past,
Even then, when from the bower I turned away,
Exulting, rich beyond the wealth of kings
I felt a sense of pain when I beheld
The silent trees and the intruding sky. –

　　Then, dearest Maiden! move along these shades
In gentleness of heart; with gentle hand
Touch, — for there is a Spirit in the woods.

BENEATH THESE FRUIT-TREE BOUGHS THAT SHED

Their snow-white blossoms on my head,

With brightest sunshine round me spread

  Of spring's unclouded weather,

In this sequestered nook how sweet

To sit upon my orchard-seat!

And birds and flowers once more to greet,

  My last year's friends together.

One have I marked, the happiest guest

In all this covert of the blest:

Hail to Thee, far above the rest

  In joy of voice and pinion!

Thou, Linnet! in thy green array,

Presiding Spirit here to-day,

Dost lead the revels of the May;

  And this is thy dominion.

While birds, and butterflies, and flowers,

Make all one band of paramours,

Thou, ranging up and down the bowers,

  Art sole in thy employment:

A Life, a Presence like the Air,

Scattering thy gladness without care,

Too blest with any one to pair;

  Thyself thy own enjoyment.

Amid yon tuft of hazel trees,

That twinkle to the gusty breeze,

Behold him perched in ecstasies,

  Yet seeming still to hover;

There! where the flutter of his wings

Upon his back and body flings

Shadows and sunny glimmerings,

  That cover him all over.

My dazzled sight he oft deceives,

A Brother of the dancing leaves;

Then flits, and from the cottage eaves

  Pours forth his song in gushes;

As if by that exulting strain

He mocked and treated with disdain

The voiceless Form he chose to feign,

  While fluttering in the bushes.

THREE YEARS SHE GREW IN SUN AND SHOWER,

Then Nature said, 'A lovelier flower
On earth was never sown;
This Child I to myself will take,
She shall be mine, and I will make
A Lady of my own.

'Myself will to my darling be
Both law and impulse, and with me
The Girl in rock and plain,
In earth and heaven, in glade and bower,
Shall feel an overseeing power
To kindle or restrain.

'She shall be sportive as the fawn
That wild with glee across the lawn
Or up the mountain springs,
And hers shall be the breathing balm,
And hers the silence and the calm
Of mute insensate things.

'The floating clouds their state shall lend
To her, for her the willow bend,
Nor shall she fail to see

Even in the motions of the storm
A beauty that shall mould her form
By silent sympathy.

'The stars of midnight shall be dear
To her, and she shall lean her ear
In many a secret place
Where rivulets dance their wayward round,
And beauty born of murmuring sound
Shall pass into her face.

'And vital feelings of delight
Shall rear her form to stately height,
Her virgin bosom swell,
Such thoughts to Lucy I will give
While she and I together live
Here in this happy dell.'

Thus Nature spake – The work was done –
How soon my Lucy's race was run!
She died and left to me
This heath, this calm and quiet scene,
The memory of what has been,
And never more will be.

Thomas Creswick

Young Girl Bathing her Feet

45

William B Hough   STILL LIFE WITH BIRD'S NEST AND PRIMROSES ON A MOSSY BANK

LOOK, FIVE BLUE EGGS ARE GLEAMING THERE!
Few visions have I seen more fair,
Nor many prospects of delight
More pleasing than that simple sight!
I started, seeming to espy
The home and sheltered bed,
The Sparrow's dwelling, which, hard by
My Father's House, in wet or dry,
My Sister Emmeline and I
    Together visited.

She looked at it as if she feared it;
Still wishing, dreading to be near it:
Such heart was in her, being then
A little Prattler among men.
The Blessing of my later years
Was with me when a Boy;
She gave me eyes, she gave me ears;
And humble cares, and delicate fears;
A heart, the fountain of sweet tears;
    And love, and thought, and joy.

To a Sky-Lark

UP WITH ME! UP WITH ME INTO THE CLOUDS!
  For thy song, Lark, is strong;
Up with me, up with me into the clouds!
  Singing, singing,
With all the heav'ns about thee ringing,
  Lift me, guide me, till I find
That spot which seems so to thy mind!

I have walked through wildernesses dreary,
  And today my heart is weary;
  Had I now the soul of a Faery,
    Up to thee would I fly.
There is madness about thee, and joy divine
  In that song of thine;
Up with me, up with me, high and high,

To thy banqueting-place in the sky!
  Joyous as Morning,
  Thou art laughing and scorning;
Thou hast a nest, for thy love and thy rest:
And, though little troubled with sloth,
Drunken Lark! thou would'st be loth
To be such a Traveller as I.
    Happy, happy Liver!
With a soul as strong as a mountain River.
Pouring out praise to the Almighty Giver,
Joy and jollity be with us both!
Hearing thee, or else some other,
    As merry a Brother,
I on the earth will go plodding on,
By myself, chearfully, till the day is done.

Sir Edwin Landseer LANDSCAPE

ODE: INTIMATIONS OF IMMORTALITY

THERE WAS A TIME WHEN MEADOW, GROVE, AND STREAM,
The earth, and every common sight,
　To me did seem
　Apparelled in celestial light,
The glory and the freshness of a dream,
It is not now as it has been of yore; –
　Turn wheresoe'er I may,
　　By night or day,
The things which I have seen I now can see no more.

　The Rainbow comes and goes,
　And lovely is the Rose,
　The Moon doth with delight
Look round her when the heavens are bare;
　Waters on a starry night
　Are beautiful and fair;
　The sunshine is a glorious birth;
　But yet I know, where'er I go,
That there hath passed away a glory from the earth.

Now, while the Birds thus sing a joyous song,
　And while the young Lambs bound
　　As to the tabor's sound,
To me alone there came a thought of grief:
A timely utterance gave that thought relief,
　And I again am strong.
The Cataracts blow their trumpets from the steep,
No more shall grief of mine the season wrong;
I hear the Echoes through the mountains throng,
The Winds come to me from the fields of sleep,
　And all the earth is gay,
　　Land and sea
　Give themselves up to jollity,
　And with the heart of May
Doth every Beast keep holiday,
　Thou Child of Joy
Shout round me, let me hear thy shouts, thou
　　　　　happy Shepherd Boy!

George Frederick Watts   THE RAINBOW

William Hall LANDSCAPE

Ye blessed Creatures, I have heard the call
　Ye to each other make; I see
The heavens laugh with you in your jubilee:
　My heart is at your festival,
　My head hath its coronal,
The fullness of your bliss, I feel – I feel it all.
　Oh evil day! if I were sullen
　While the Earth herself is adorning,
　　This sweet May-morning,
　And the Children are pulling,
　　On every side,
　In a thousand vallies far and wide,
　Fresh flowers; while the sun shines warm,
And the Babe leaps up on his mother's arm: –
　I hear, I hear, with joy I hear!
　– But there's a Tree, of many, one,
A single Field which I have looked upon,
Both of them speak of something that is gone:
　　The Pansy at my feet
　　Doth the same tale repeat:
Whither is fled the visionary gleam?
Where is it now, the glory and the dream?

Our birth is but a sleep and a forgetting:
The Soul that rises with us, our life's Star,

Hath had elsewhere its setting,
　And cometh from afar:
　Not in entire forgetfulness,
　And not in utter nakedness,
But trailing clouds of glory do we come
　　From God, who is our home:
Heaven lies about us in our infancy!
Shades of the prison-house begin to close
　　Upon the growing Boy,
But He beholds the light, and whence it flows,
　　He sees it in his joy;
The Youth, who daily farther from the East
　Must travel, still is Nature's Priest,
　　And by the vision splendid
　　Is on his way attended;
At length the Man perceives it die away,
And fade into the light of common day.

Earth fills her lap with pleasures of her own;
Yearnings she hath in her own natural kind,

And, even with something of a Mother's mind,
    And no unworthy aim
    The homely Nurse doth all she can
To make her Foster-child, her Inmate Man,
    Forget the glories he hath known,
And that imperial palace whence he came.

Behold the Child among his new-born blisses,
A four year's Darling of a pigmy size!
See, where 'mid work of his own hand he lies,
Fretted by sallies of his Mother's kisses,
With light upon him from his Father's eyes!
See, at his feet, some little plan or chart,
Some fragment from his dream of human life,
Shaped by himself with newly-learned art;
    A wedding or a festival,
    A mourning or a funeral;
      And this hath now his heart,
    And unto this he frames his song:
      Then will he fit his tongue
To dialogues of business, love, or strife;
    But it will not be long
    Ere this be thrown aside,
    And with new joy and pride
The little Actor cons another part,

Filling from time to time his 'humorous stage'
With all the Persons, down to palsied Age,
That Life brings with her in her Equipage;
    As if his whole vocation
    Were endless imitation.

Thou, whose exterior semblance doth belie
    Thy Soul's immensity;
Thou best Philosopher, who yet dost keep
Thy heritage, thou Eye among the blind,
That, deaf and silent, read'st the eternal deep,
Haunted for ever by the eternal mind, –
    Mighty Prophet! Seer blest!
    On whom those truths do rest,
Which we are toiling all our lives to find;
Thou, over whom thy Immortality
Broods like the Day, a Master o'er a Slave,
A Presence which is not to be put by;
    To whom the grave
Is but a lonely bed without the sense or sight
    Of day or the warm light,
A place of thought where we in waiting lie;
Thou little Child, yet glorious in the might
Of untamed pleasures, on thy Being's height,
Why with such earnest pains dost thou provoke

The Years to bring the inevitable yoke,
Thus blindly with thy blessedness at strife?
Full soon thy Soul shall have her earthly freight,
And custom lie upon thee with a weight,
Heavy as frost, and deep almost as life!

O joy! that in our embers
Is something that doth live,
That nature yet remembers
What was so fugitive!
The thought of our past years in me doth breed
Perpetual benedictions: not indeed
For that which is most worthy to be blest;
Delight and liberty, the simple creed
Of Childhood, whether fluttering or at rest,
With new-born hope for ever in his breast: –
Not for these I raise
The song of thanks and praise;
But for those obstinate questionings
Of sense and outward things,
Fallings from us, vanishings;
Blank misgivings of a Creature
Moving about in worlds not realized,
High instincts, before which our mortal Nature
Did tremble like a guilty Thing surprised:

But for those first affections,
Those shadowy recollections,
Which, be they what they may,
Are yet the fountain light of all our day,
Are yet a master light of all our seeing;
Uphold us, cherish us, and make
Our noisy years seem moments in the being
Of the eternal Silence: truths that wake,
To perish never;
Which neither listlessness, nor mad endeavour,
Nor Man nor Boy,
Nor all that is at enmity with joy,
Can utterly abolish or destroy!
Hence, in a season of calm weather,
Though inland far we be,
Our Souls have sight of that immortal sea
Which brought us hither,
Can in a moment travel thither,
And see the Children sport upon the shore,
And hear the mighty waters rolling evermore.

Then, sing ye Birds, sing, sing a joyous song!
And let the young Lambs bound
As to the tabor's sound!
We in thought will join your throng,

Ye that pipe and ye that play,
Ye that through your hearts today
Feel the gladness of the May!
What though the radiance which was once so bright
Be now for ever taken from my sight,
Though nothing can bring back the hour
Of splendour in the grass, of glory in the flower;
We will grieve not, rather find
Strength in what remains behind,
In the primal sympathy
Which having been must ever be,
In the soothing thoughts that spring
Out of human suffering,
In the faith that looks through death,
In years that bring the philosophic mind.

And oh ye Fountains, Meadow, Hills, and Groves,
Think not of any severing of our loves!
Yet in my heart of hearts I feel your might;
I only have relinquished one delight
To live beneath your more habitual sway.
I love the Brooks which down their channels fret,
Even more than when I tripped lightly as they;
The innocent brightness of a new-born Day
Is lovely yet;
The Clouds that gather round the setting sun
Do take a sober colouring from an eye
That hath kept watch o'er man's mortality;
Another race hath been, and other palms are won.
Thanks to the human heart by which we live,
Thanks to its tenderness, its joys, and fears,
To me the meanest flower that blows can give
Thoughts that do often lie too deep for tears.

William Havell   WETHERLAND FROM LITTLE LANGDALE

Elegiac Stanzas

Suggested by a Picture of Peele Castle, in a Storm,
Painted by Sir George Beaumont

I WAS THY NEIGHBOUR ONCE, THOU RUGGED PILE!
Four summer weeks I dwelt in sight of thee:
I saw thee every day; and all the while
Thy Form was sleeping on a glassy sea.

So pure the sky, so quiet was the air!
So like, so very like, was day to day!
Whene'er I looked, thy Image still was there;
It trembled, but it never passed away.

How perfect was the calm! it seemed no sleep;
No mood, which season takes away, or brings:
I could have fancied that the mighty Deep
Was even the gentlest of all gentle Things.

Ah! THEN, if mine had been the Painter's hand,
To express what then I saw; and add the gleam,
The light that never was, on sea or land,
The consecration, and the Poet's dream;

I would have planted thee, thou hoary Pile!
Amid a world how different from this!
Beside a sea that could not cease to smile;
On tranquil land, beneath a sky of bliss:

Thou shouldst have seemed a treasure-house, a mine
Of peaceful years; a chronicle of heaven:–
Of all the sunbeams that did ever shine
The very sweetest had to thee been given.

A Picture had it been of lasting ease,
Elysian quiet, without toil or strife;
No motion but the moving tide, a breeze,
Or merely silent Nature's breathing life.

Such, in the fond delusion of my heart,
Such Picture would I at that time have made:
And seen the soul of truth in every part;
A faith, a trust, that could not be betrayed.

George Beaumont   Castle in a Storm

So once it would have been, – 'tis so no more;
I have submitted to a new controul:
A power is gone, which nothing can restore;
A deep distress hath humanized my Soul.

Not for a moment could I now behold
A smiling sea and be what I have been:
The feeling of my loss will ne'er be old;
This, which I know, I speak with mind serene.

Then, Beaumont, Friend! who would have been
   the Friend,
If he had lived, of Him whom I deplore,
This Work of thine I blame not, but commend;
This sea in anger, and the dismal shore.

Oh 'tis a passionate Work! – yet wise and well;
Well chosen is the spirit that is here;
That Hulk which labours in the deadly swell,
This rueful sky, this pageantry of fear!

And this huge Castle, standing here sublime,
I love to see the look with which it braves,
Cased in the unfeeling armour of old time,
The light'ning, the fierce wind, and trampling waves.

Farewell, farewell the Heart that lives alone,
Housed in a dream, at distance from the Kind!
Such happiness, wherever it be known
Is to be pitied; for 'tis surely blind.

But welcome fortitude, and patient chear,
And frequent sights of what is to be borne!
Such sights, or worse, as are before me here. –
Not without hope we suffer and we mourn.

O NIGHTINGALE! THOU SURELY ART

A Creature of a fiery heart –
These notes of thine they pierce, and pierce;
Tumultuous harmony and fierce!
Thou sing'st as if the God of wine
Had helped thee to a Valentine;
A song in mockery and despite
Of shades, and dews, and silent Night,
And steady bliss, and all the Loves
Now sleeping in these peaceful groves!

I heard a Stockdove sing or say
His homely tale, this very day.
His voice was buried among trees,
Yet to be come at by the breeze:
He did not cease; but cooed – and cooed;
And somewhat pensively he wooed:
He sang of love with quiet blending,
Slow to begin, and never ending;
Of serious faith, and inward glee;
That was the Song, the Song for me!

SHE DWELT AMONG TH' UNTRODDEN WAYS

    Beside the springs of Dove,

A Maid whom there were none to praise

    And very few to love.

A Violet by a mossy stone

    Half-hidden from the Eye!

– Fair, as a star when only one

    Is shining in the sky!

She *lived* unknown, and few could know

    When Lucy ceased to be;

But she is in her Grave, and Oh!

    The difference to me.

Frederick William Hulme   A Path Through the Meadows

William Bell Scott   A Seashore at Sunset

IT IS A BEAUTEOUS EVENING, CALM AND FREE;

The holy time is quiet as a Nun

Breathless with adoration; the broad sun

Is sinking down in its tranquillity;

The gentleness of heaven broods o'er the Sea:

Listen! the mighty Being is awake

And doth with his eternal motion make

A sound like thunder – everlastingly.

Dear Child! dear Girl! that walkest with me here,

If thou appear'st untouched by solemn thought,

Thy nature is not therefore less divine:

Thou liest in Abraham's bosom all the year;

And worshipp'st at the Temple's inner shrine,

God being with thee when we know it not.

CALM IS THE FRAGRANT AIR, AND LOTH TO LOSE

Day's grateful warmth, tho' moist with falling dews.

Look for the stars, you'll say that there are none;

Look up a second time, and, one by one,

You mark them twinkling out with silvery light,

And wonder how they could elude the sight.

The birds, of late so noisy in their bowers,

Warbled a while with faint and fainter powers,

But now are silent as the dim-seen flowers:

Nor does the Village Church-clock's iron tone

The time's and season's influence disown;

Nine beats distinctly to each other bound

In drowsy sequence; how unlike the sound

That, in rough winter, oft inflicts a fear

On fireside Listeners, doubting what they hear!

The Shepherd, bent on rising with the sun,

Had closed his door before the day was done,

And now with thankful heart to bed doth creep,

And join his little Children in their sleep.

The Bat, lured forth where trees the lane o'ershade,

Flits and reflits along the close arcade;

Far-heard the Dor-hawk chases the white Moth

With burring note, which Industry and Sloth

Might both be pleased with, for it suits them both.

Wheels and the tread of hoofs are heard no more;

One Boat there was, but it will touch the shore

With the next dipping of its slackened oar;

Faint sound, that, for the gayest of the gay,

Might give to serious thought a moment's sway,

As a last token of Man's toilsome day!

66

John Sell Cotman   POSTWICK GROVE

Joshua Anderson Hague LANDSCAPE

BEHOLD HER, SINGLE IN THE FIELD,
Yon solitary Highland Lass!
Reaping and singing by herself;
Stop here, or gently pass!
Alone she cuts, and binds the grain,
And sings a melancholy strain;
O listen! for the Vale profound
Is overflowing with the sound.

No Nightingale did ever chaunt
So sweetly to reposing bands
Of Travellers in some shady haunt,
Among Arabian Sands:
No sweeter voice was ever heard
In spring-time from the Cuckoo-bird,
Breaking the silence of the seas
Among the farthest Hebrides.

Will no one tell me what she sings?
Perhaps the plaintive numbers flow
For old, unhappy, far-off things,
And battles long ago:
Or is it some more humble lay,
Familiar matter of today?
Some natural sorrow, loss, or pain,
That has been, and may be again!

Whate'er the theme, the Maiden sang
As if her song could have no ending;
I saw her singing at her work,
And o'er the sickle bending;
I listened, motionless and still;
And, as I mounted up the hill,
The music in my heart I bore,
Long after it was heard no more.

ODE: COMPOSED UPON AN EVENING OF EXTRAORDINARY SPLENDOUR AND BEAUTY

I

HAD THIS EFFULGENCE DISAPPEARED

With flying haste, I might have sent
Among the speechless clouds a look
Of blank astonishment;
But 'tis endued with power to stay,
And sanctify one closing day,
That frail Mortality may see,
What is? – ah no, but what *can* be!
Time was when field and watery cove
With modulated echoes rang,
While choirs of fervent Angels sang
Their vespers in the grove;
Or, ranged like stars along some sovereign height,
Warbled, for heaven above and earth below,
Strains suitable to both. – Such holy rite,
Methinks, if audibly repeated now
From hill or valley, could not move
Sublimer transport, purer love,
Than doth this silent spectacle – the gleam –
The shadow – and the peace supreme!

II

No sound is uttered, – but a deep
And solemn harmony pervades
The hollow vale from steep to steep,
And penetrates the glades.
Far-distant images draw nigh,
Called forth by wond'rous potency
Of beamy radiance, that imbues
Whate'er it strikes, with gem-like hues!
In vision exquisitely clear,
Herds range along the mountain side;
And glistening antlers are descried;
And gilded flocks appear.
Thine is the tranquil hour, purpureal Eve!
But long as god-like wish, or hope divine,
Informs my spirit, ne'er can I believe
That this magnificence is wholly thine!
– From worlds not quickened by the sun
A portion of the gift is won;
An intermingling of Heaven's pomp is spread
On ground which British shepherds tread!

James Thomas Linnell   THE RAINBOW

Joseph Wright of Derby   Ullswater

III

And, if there be whom broken ties

Afflict, or injuries assail,

Yon hazy ridges to their eyes,

Present a glorious scale,

Climbing suffused with sunny air,

To stop – no record hath told where!

And tempting fancy to ascend,

And with immortal spirits blend!

– Wings at my shoulder seem to play;

But, rooted here, I stand and gaze

Oh those bright steps that heaven-ward raise

Their practicable way.

Come forth, ye drooping old men, look abroad

And see to what fair countries ye are bound!

And if some Traveller, weary of his road,

Hath slept since noon-tide on the grassy ground,

Ye Genii! to his covert speed;

And wake him with such gentle heed

As may attune his soul to meet the dow'r

Bestowed on this transcendent hour!

IV

Such hues from their celestial Urn

Were wont to stream before my eye,

Where'er it wandered in the morn

Of blissful infancy.

This glimpse of glory, why renewed?

Nay, rather speak with gratitude;

For, if a vestige of those gleams

Survived, 'twas only in my dreams.

Dread Power! whom peace and calmness serve

No less than Nature's threatening voice,

If aught unworthy be my choice,

From THEE if I would swerve,

O, let thy grace remind me of the light,

Full early lost and fruitlessly deplored;

Which, at this moment, on my waking sight

Appears to shine, by miracle restored!

My soul, though yet confined to earth,

Rejoices in a second birth;

– 'Tis past, the visionary splendour fades,

And Night approaches with her shades.

To a Butterfly I

I'VE WATCHED YOU NOW A FULL HALF HOUR,

Self-poised upon that yellow flower;
And, little Butterfly! indeed
I know not if you sleep, or feed.
How motionless! not frozen seas
More motionless! and then
What joy awaits you, when the breeze
Hath found you out among the trees,
And calls you forth again!

This plot of Orchard-ground is ours;
My trees they are, my Sister's flowers;
Stop here whenever you are weary,
And rest as in a sanctuary!
Come often to us, fear no wrong;
Sit near us on the bough!
We'll talk of sunshine and of song;
And summer days, when we were young,
Sweet childish days, that were as long
        As twenty days are now!

To a Butterfly II

STAY NEAR ME – DO NOT TAKE THY FLIGHT!

A little longer stay in sight!
Much converse do I find in Thee,
Historian of my Infancy!
Float near me; do not yet depart!
Dead times revive in thee:
Thou bring'st, gay Creature as thou art!
A solemn image to my heart,
My Father's Family!

Oh! pleasant, pleasant were the days,
The time, when in our childish plays
My sister Emmeline and I
Together chased the Butterfly!
A very hunter did I rush
Upon the prey: – with leaps and springs
I followed on from brake to bush;
But She, God love her! feared to brush
The dust from off its wings.

Thomas Worsey   PRIMROSES, POLYANTHUS, APPLE BLOSSOM AND A BIRD'S NEST ON A MOSSY BANK

FAREWELL, THOU LITTLE NOOK OF MOUNTAIN GROUND,

Thou rocky corner in the lowest stair
Of that magnificent temple which doth bound
One side of our whole vale with grandeur rare,
Sweet garden-orchard! eminently fair,
The loveliest spot that man hath ever found.
Farewell! we leave thee to Heaven's peaceful care.
Thee, and the Cottage which thou dost surround.

Our Boat is safely anchored by the shore:
And there will safely ride when we are gone:
The flowering shrubs that deck our humble door
Will prosper, though untended and alone;
Fields, goods, and far off chattels we have none;
These narrow bounds contain our private store
Of things earth makes, and sun doth shine upon;
Here are they in our sight: we have no more.

Sunshine and showers be with you, bud and bell!
For two months now in vain we shall be sought:
We leave you here in solitude to dwell
With these our latest gifts of tender thought,
Thou, like the morning in thy saffron coat
Bright gowan! and marsh-marygold, farewell!
Whom from the borders of the Lake we brought
And placed together near our rocky Well.

We go for One to whom ye will be dear;
And she will prize this Bower, this Indian shed,
Our own contrivance, Building without peer:
A gentle Maid! whose heart is lowly bred,
Whose pleasures are in wild fields gathered;
With joyousness, and with a thoughtful cheer
Will come to you; to you herself will wed;
And love the blessed life that we lead here.

George Beaumont Applethwaite

Henry Clarence Whaite   Castle Rock (Cumberland)

Dear Spot! whom we have watched with tender
   heed,
Bringing thee chosen plants and blossoms blown
Among the distant mountains, flower and weed
Which thou hast taken to thee as thy own,
Making all kindness registered and known;
Thou for our sakes, though Nature's Child indeed,
Fair in thyself and beautiful alone,
Hast taken gifts which thou dost little need;

And, O most constant, yet most fickle Place!
That hast thy wayward moods, as thou dost show
To them who look not daily on thy face,
Who, being loved, in love no bounds dost know,
And say'st when we forsake thee, 'Let them go!'
Thou easy-hearted Thing! with thy wild race
Of weeds and flowers, till we return be slow,
And travel with the year at a soft pace:

Help us to tell Her tales of years gone by,
And this sweet spring the best beloved and best;
Joy will be flown in its mortality,
Something must stay to tell us of the rest,
Here thronged with primroses, the steep rock's
   breast
Glittered at evening like a starry sky;
And in this bush our sparrow built its nest,
Of which I sang one song that will not die.

O happy Garden! whose seclusion deep
Hath been so friendly to industrious hours.
And to soft slumbers, that did gently steep
Our spirits, carrying with them dreams of flowers,
And wild notes warbled among leafy bowers;
Two burning months let summer overleap,
And, coming back with Her who will be ours,
Into thy bosom we again shall creep.

NUNS FRET NOT AT THEIR CONVENT'S NARROW ROOM;

And Hermits are contented with their Cells;

And Students with their pensive Citadels:

Maids at the Wheel, the Weaver at his Loom,

Sit blithe and happy; Bees that soar for bloom,

High as the highest Peak of Furness Fells,

Will murmur by the hour in Foxglove bells:

In truth, the prison, unto which we doom

Ourselves, no prison is: and hence for me,

In sundry moods, 'twas pastime to be bound

Within the Sonnet's scanty plot of ground:

Pleased if some Souls (for such there needs must be)

Who have felt the weight of too much liberty,

Should find short solace there, as I have found.

Edmund George Warren   SHEEP IN A WOODED LANDSCAPE

I WANDERED LONELY AS A CLOUD

That floats on high o'er vales and hills,
When all at once I saw a crowd,
A host, of golden daffodils;
Beside the lake, beneath the trees,
Fluttering and dancing in the breeze.

Continuous as the stars that shine
And twinkle on the milky way,
They stretched in never-ending line
Along the margin of a bay:
Ten thousand saw I at a glance,
Tossing their heads in sprightly dance.

The waves beside them danced; but they
Out-did the sparkling waves in glee:
A poet could not but be gay,
In such a jocund company:
I gazed – and gazed – but little thought
What wealth the show to me had brought:

For oft, when on my couch I lie
In vacant or in pensive mood,
They flash upon that inward eye
Which is the bliss of solitude;
And then my heart with pleasure fills,
And dances with the daffodils.

THE SMALL CELANDINE

THERE IS A FLOWER, THE LESSER CELANDINE,
That shrinks, like many more, from cold and rain;
And, the first moment that the sun may shine,
Bright as the sun itself, 'tis out again!

When hailstones have been falling swarm on swarm,
Or blasts the green field and the trees distressed,
Oft have I seen it muffled up from harm,
In close self-shelter, like a Thing at rest.

But lately, one rough day, this Flower I passed,
And recognized it, though an altered Form,
Now standing forth an offering to the Blast,
And buffetted at will by Rain and Storm.

I stopped, and said with inly muttered voice,
'It doth not love the shower, nor seek the cold:
This neither is its courage nor its choice,
But its necessity in being old.

The sunshine may not bless it, nor the dew;
It cannot help itself in its decay;
Stiff in its members, withered, changed of hue.'
And, in my spleen, I smiled that it was grey.

To be a Prodigal's Favourite – then, worse truth,
A Miser's Pensioner – behold our lot!
O Man! that from thy fair and shining youth
Age might but take the things Youth needed not!

MY HEART LEAPS UP WHEN I BEHOLD

A Rainbow in the sky:

So was it when my life began;

So is it now I am a Man;

So be it when I shall grow old,

Or let me die!

The Child is Father of the Man;

And I could wish my days to be

Bound each to each by natural piety.

Joseph Wright of Derby   Landscape with a Rainbow

Among all lovely things my love had been;

Had noted well the stars, all flowers that grew

About her home; but she had never seen

A Glow-worm, never one, and this I knew.

While riding near her home one stormy night

A single Glow-worm did I chance to espy;

I gave a fervent welcome to the sight,

And from my Horse I leapt; great joy had I.

Upon a leaf the Glow-worm did I lay,

To bear it with me through the stormy night:

And, as before, it shone without dismay;

Albeit putting forth a fainter light.

When to the Dwelling of my Love I came,

I went into the Orchard quietly;

And left the Glow-worm, blessing it by name,

Laid safely by itself, beneath a Tree.

The whole next day, I hoped, and hoped with fear;

At night the Glow-worm shone beneath the Tree:

I led my Lucy to the spot, 'Look here!'

Oh! joy it was for her, and joy for me!

STRANGE FITS OF PASSION I HAVE KNOWN,
And I will dare to tell,
But in the lover's ear alone,
What once to me befel.

When she I loved, was strong and gay
And like a rose in June,
I to her cottage bent my way,
Beneath the evening moon.

Upon the moon I fixed my eye
All over the wide lea;
My horse trudged on, and we drew nigh
Those paths so dear to me.

And now we reached the orchard plot,
And, as we climbed the hill,
Towards the roof of Lucy's cot
The moon descended still.

In one of those sweet dreams I slept,
Kind Nature's gentlest boon!
And, all the while, my eyes I kept
On the descending moon.

My horse moved on; hoof after hoof
He raised and never stopped:
When down behind the cottage roof
At once the planet dropped.

What fond and wayward thoughts will slide
Into a Lover's head –
'O mercy!' to myself I cried,
'If Lucy should be dead!'

'BEGONE, THOU FOND PRESUMPTUOUS ELF,'

Exclaimed an angry Voice,

'Nor dare to thrust thy foolish self

Between me and my choice!'

A small Cascade fresh swoln with snows

Thus threatened a poor Briar-rose,

That, all bespattered with his foam,

And dancing high, and dancing low,

Was living, as a child might know,

In an unhappy home.

'Dost thou presume my course to block?

Off, off! or, puny Thing!

I'll hurl thee headlong with the rock

To which thy fibres cling.'

The Flood was tyrannous and strong;

The patient Briar suffered long,

Nor did he utter groan or sigh,

Hoping the danger would be passed:

But seeing no relief, at last

He ventured to reply.

'Ah!' said the Briar, 'Blame me not!

Why should we dwell in strife?

We who in this sequestered spot,

Once lived a happy life!

You stirred me on my rocky bed –

What pleasure through my veins you spread

The Summer long, from day to day

My leaves you freshened and bedewed;

Nor was it common gratitude

That did your cares repay.

'When Spring came on with bud and bell,

Among these rocks did I

Before you hang my wreaths to tell

John Brandon Smith RUTHVEN FALLS

That gentle days were nigh!
And in the sultry summer hours
I sheltered you with leaves and flowers;
And in my leaves – now shed and gone,
The linnet lodged, and for us two
Chanted his pretty songs, when you
Had little voice or none.

'But now proud thoughts are in your breast –
What grief is mine you see.
Ah! would you think even yet how blest
Together we might be!
Though of both leaf and flower bereft,

Some ornaments to me are left –
Rich store of scarlet hips is mine,
With which I, in my humble way
Would deck you many a Winter day,
A happy Eglantine!'

What more he said I cannot tell,
The Torrent down the rocky dell
Came thundering loud and fast;
I listened, nor aught else could hear,
The Briar quaked – and much I fear
Those accents were his last.

Peter de Wint FALLS OF THE WEST LYNN

I MET LOUISA IN THE SHADE;
And, having seen that lovely Maid,
Why should I fear to say
That she is ruddy, fleet, and strong;
And down the rocks can leap along,
Like rivulets in May?

And she hath smiles to earth unknown;
Smiles, that with motion of their own
Do spread, and sink, and rise;
That come and go with endless play,
And ever, as they pass away,
Are hidden in her eyes.

She loves her fire, her Cottage-home;
Yet o'er the moorland will she roam
In weather rough and bleak;
And when against the wind she strains,
Oh! might I kiss the mountain rains.
That sparkle on her cheek.

Take all that's mine 'beneath the moon,'
If I with her but half a noon
May sit beneath the walls
Of some old cave, or mossy nook,
When up she winds along the brook,
To hunt the waterfalls.

Benjamin William Leader Landscape with a Young Woman

PANSIES, LILIES, KINGCUPS, DAISIES,
Let them live upon their praises;
Long as there's a sun that sets,
Primroses will have their glory;
Long as there are violets,
They will have a place in story:
There's a flower that shall be mine,
'Tis the little Celandine.

Eyes of some men travel far
For the finding of a star;
Up and down the heavens they go,
Men that keep a mighty rout!
I'm as great as they, I trow,
Since the day I found thee out,
Little Flower – I'll make a stir,
Like a sage astronomer.

Modest, yet withal an Elf
Bold, and lavish of thyself;

Since we needs must first have met
I have seen thee, high and low,
Thirty years or more, and yet
'Twas a face I did not know;
Thou hast now, go where I may,
Fifty greetings in a day.

Ere a leaf is on a bush,
In the time before the thrush
Has a thought about her nest,
Thou wilt come with half a call,
Spreading out thy glossy breast
Like a careless Prodigal;
Telling tales about the sun,
When we've little warmth, or none.

Poets, vain men in their mood!
Travel with the multitude:
Never heed them; I aver
That they all are wanton wooers;

But the thrifty cottager,
Who stirs little out of doors,
Joys to spy thee near her home;
Spring is coming, Thou art come!

Comfort have thou of thy merit,
Kindly, unassuming Spirit!
Careless of thy neighbourhood,
Thou dost show thy pleasant face
On the moor, and in the wood,
In the lane; – there's not a place,
Howsoever mean it be,
But 'tis good enough for thee.

Ill befall the yellow flowers,
Children of the flaring hours!
Buttercups, that will be seen,
Whether we will see or no;
Others, too, of lofty mien;
They have done as worldlings do,
Taken praise that should be thine,
Little, humble Celandine.

Prophet of delight and mirth,
Ill-requited upon earth;
Herald of a mighty band,
Of a joyous train ensuing,
Serving at my heart's command,
Tasks that are no tasks renewing,
I will sing, as doth behove,
Hymns in praise of what I love!

ACKNOWLEDGEMENTS

Ackermann and Johnson Ltd, London/Bridgeman Art Library, *page 21.*
Birmingham City Art Gallery, *page 39.*
Bonhams, London/Bridgeman Art Library, *page 63.*
British Museum, London, *page 26.*
Carlisle Museum and Art Gallery, *page 14.*
Christie's Images, *pages 2, 37, 46, 72, 75 and 91.*
Christie's, London/Bridgeman Art Library, *page 32.*
Derby Museum and Art Gallery/Giraudon/Bridgeman Art Library, *page 85.*
Fine Art Society, London/Bridgeman Art Library, *page 51.*
Fitzwilliam Museum, Cambridge, *pages 18 and 67.*
Forbes Magazine Collection, New York/Bridgeman Art Library, *page 71.*
Leicestershire Museums, Arts and Records Service, *pages 59 and 77.*
Manchester City Art Galleries, *page 68.*
Roy Miles Gallery, London/Bridgeman Art Library, *pages 40, 49, and 93.*
John Noott Galleries, Worcester/Bridgeman Art Library, *page 17.*
Phillips, London/Bridgeman Art Library, *page 45.*
Reading Museum and Art Gallery, *page 57.*
Royal Albert Memorial Museum, Exeter/Bridgeman Art Library, *page 25.*
Sotheby's, London, *pages 31, 64, 81 and 88.*
Tate Gallery, London, *cover.*
Victoria and Albert Museum, London/Bridgeman Art Library, *page 52.*
Walker Art Gallery, (Board of Trustees of the National Museums and Galleries on Merseyside),
Liverpool, *pages 13 and 78.*
York City Art Gallery/Bridgeman Art Library, *page 6.*

PICTURE RESEARCH: GABRIELLE ALLEN

*The publishers have made every effort to trace the copyright-holders, but if they have
inadvertently overlooked any, they will be pleased to make the necessary arrangement at the
first opportunity.*